Samuel French Acting Edition

Dramatic Debuts
Volume 1

Writer's Block
by Samuel French

Mechant Enfant
by Samuel Mayer

The Metronome
by Gabriel Neustadt

Unwanted Adventure
by Brandon Johnson

SAMUELFRENCH.COM   SAMUELFRENCH.CO.UK

Writer's Block Copyright © 2009 by Samuel French
Mechant Enfant Copyright © 2009 by Samuel Mayer
The Metronome Copyright © 2009 by Gabriel Neustadt
Unwanted Adventure Copyright © 2009 by Brandon Johnson
All Rights Reserved

DRAMATIC DEBUTS is fully protected under the copyright laws of the United States of America, the British Commonwealth, including Canada, and all other countries of the Copyright Union. All rights, including professional and amateur stage productions, recitation, lecturing, public reading, motion picture, radio broadcasting, television and the rights of translation into foreign languages are strictly reserved.

ISBN 978-0-874-40223-0

www.SamuelFrench.com
www.SamuelFrench.co.uk

For Production Enquiries

United States and Canada
Info@SamuelFrench.com
1-866-598-8449

United Kingdom and Europe
Plays@SamuelFrench.co.uk
020-7255-4302

Each title is subject to availability from Samuel French, depending upon country of performance. Please be aware that *DRAMATIC DEBUTS* may not be licensed by Samuel French in your territory. Professional and amateur producers should contact the nearest Samuel French office or licensing partner to verify availability.

CAUTION: Professional and amateur producers are hereby warned that *DRAMATIC DEBUTS* is subject to a licensing fee. Publication of this play(s) does not imply availability for performance. Both amateurs and professionals considering a production are strongly advised to apply to Samuel French before starting rehearsals, advertising, or booking a theatre. A licensing fee must be paid whether the title(s) is presented for charity or gain and whether or not admission is charged. Professional/Stock licensing fees are quoted upon application to Samuel French.

No one shall make any changes in this title(s) for the purpose of production. No part of this book may be reproduced, stored in a retrieval system, or transmitted in any form, by any means, now known or yet to be invented, including mechanical, electronic, photocopying, recording, videotaping, or otherwise, without the prior written permission of the publisher. No one shall upload this title(s), or part of this title(s), to any social media websites.

For all enquiries regarding motion picture, television, and other media rights, please contact Samuel French.

MUSIC USE NOTE

Licensees are solely responsible for obtaining formal written permission from copyright owners to use copyrighted music in the performance of this play and are strongly cautioned to do so. If no such permission is obtained by the licensee, then the licensee must use only original music that the licensee owns and controls. Licensees are solely responsible and liable for all music clearances and shall indemnify the copyright owners of the play(s) and their licensing agent, Samuel French, against any costs, expenses, losses and liabilities arising from the use of music by licensees. Please contact the appropriate music licensing authority in your territory for the rights to any incidental music.

IMPORTANT BILLING AND CREDIT REQUIREMENTS

If you have obtained performance rights to this title, please refer to your licensing agreement for important billing and credit requirements.

THE BAKER'S PLAYS HIGH SCHOOL
PLAYWRITING COMPETITION

Baker's Plays was a strong advocate for theater in schools for over one hundred years. In the spirit of that commitment, this playwriting competition was offered for High School students. Plays may be about any subject and of any length. It is our hope that this competition has encouraged aspiring high school authors to explore the creative possibilities of writing for the stage.

This volume of *Dramatic Debuts* represents the culmination of the 2008 competition. The four short plays included in this book display what we at Baker's Plays felt was the strongest understanding of writing for the stage. The plays included in this volume are:

First Place
Writer's Block by Samuel French

Second Place
Mechant Enfant by Samuel Mayer

Third Place
The Metronome by Gabriel Neustadt

Honorable Mention
Unwanted Adventure by Brandon Johnson

We congratulate these four writers and thank all who participated in the 2008 competition.

WRITER'S BLOCK

By Samuel French

CHARACTERS

ALECK CHANCEY - A 24 year-old children's author who is suffering from depression and/or writer's block. He is young and cynical, depressed but not depressing, and at a loss for what to do.

DANNY BROOKS - Aleck's 32 year-old Agent/roommate. He is - at heart - a good friend to Aleck, but does not show it in the conventional way. He has a twisted sense of humor and doesn't take anything, especially not Aleck, seriously. The audience should never mistake his insensitivity for a lack of caring for Aleck.

TEDDY GEISEL - A drug-induced vision of a beloved children's author, who has taken a turn for the worse.

SYNOPSIS

A dark comedy about suicide, success, and Dr. Seuss. A children's author, Aleck, is dealing with a case of depression that is only made worse by his insensitive agent, Danny. The depression turns more severe as he struggles to overcome his writer's block, and to produce material for Danny. Unable to handle his life, Aleck tries to kill himself by overdosing on Advil and meets Teddy, a drug induced vision of a burn out Dr. Seuss. Teddy reminisces with Aleck about where his life went wrong, tries to convince Aleck to take drugs, and reminds Aleck why he first wanted to write children's books in the first place.

PREVIOUS PRODUCTION

Directed by Stefanie Lehmann

ALECK . . . . Ian Gabriel Gonzalez Muentener
DANNY . . . . Sierra Brown
TEDDY . . . . Nick Orfanella

*(The stage is set with a desk, a couch, and a large bookshelf that is placed, upstage, by the front door. Lights come up revealing **ALECK** and the room cluttered with books and crumpled up balls of paper. **ALECK** is writing out loud at his desk, in a very matter-of-fact tone.)*

ALECK. This is a suicide note. It was a grocery list, but as I got down to peanut butter I began thinking, "What's the point?" ...Peanut butter can do that. It's damn depressing...So if you're reading this then please disregard "shaving cream, lettuce, eggs..." and skip to right below Jif-extra crunchy.

*(**ALECK** begins to pace around the room, reading the paper out loud as if he were editing it in his head.)*

ALECK. Dear Concerned Readers and Unconcerned Onlookers,

The blame for my untimely suicide does not fall on just one solitary person. Many people are at fault. First off, my parents for their injustices against me. You were the two that first put it into my head that life was a race not worth running. I really did listen to you. Second off, my agent/roommate – Danny Brooks. I am sorry I could not write my children's books fast enough for you. Third, my Labrador Retriever, Bandit. You left me alone in this world when you ran away...and got hit by a truck. Finally, the truck driver who hit Bandit. You're an asshole.

With regrets, Aleck Chancey.

*(**DANNY**, 32, enters from offstage.)*

DANNY. What's that you're writing?

ALECK. ...grocery list.

DANNY. Don't forget peanut butter...you see, I thought it might have been a story.

ALECK. Sorry.

DANNY. Something publishable. Something the kids would like.

ALECK. I think the onion is a remarkably likable guy. So much depth. So much passion. So many lay-

DANNY. Don't say layers. Please. *(pause)* And the point is that *I'm* not screwing around here, Aleck. Two years out of college, and you're already suffering from writer's block.

ALECK. Depression.

DANNY. I keep telling you, it's writer s block. Not depression. And it's all in your head.

ALECK. So you tell me.

DANNY. And I can't find publishers for you if you can't write something. So I'd like you to stop what you're doing, sit down, and *write*.

ALECK. I can't. I'm too busy…too preoccupied.

DANNY. Doing what?

ALECK. Writing.

DANNY. Writing a grocery list.

ALECK. Suicide note, actually.

DANNY. …No, that doesn't translate well for the kids. Maybe Dr. Seuss could have accomplished it. But I don't think my six-year-old niece wants to hear about your pre-pre-mid-life crisis and she certainly doesn't wanna see the illustrations that go along.

ALECK. I'm not kidding.

DANNY. Of course you're not. What kind of a sick bastard jokes about suicide?

ALECK. Hard to imagine.

DANNY. …Don't do it.

ALECK. Why not?

DANNY. Because you haven't written the best-selling picture book of our time…yet. And you could! You've got creativity, smarts, and a small enough vocabulary for kids to understand. You could be great. But you're going to let some little hiccup of a writer's block on your road to greatness stop you? Not as long as I'm your agent – and your friend – you're not.

ALECK. "I will not off myself" was not in the contract, Danny.

DANNY. You just didn't read the fine print.

ALECK. …you're a jerk. You know that?

DANNY. Yes, and I also have a natural flair for getting talented writers, like yourself, noticed. So here's the deal. Give me one great story. Just one. And after that, I'll do anything. I'll even tie the noose.

ALECK. I'm sorry. I can't. I'm not in the right place.

DANNY. Place? What's place to do with it. I'll give you a pencil, a desk, what more do you need?

ALECK. I mean I'm not in the right mood.

DANNY. How so?

ALECK. Well it's hard to write a children's book when all I can think about is throwing myself off the roof.

DANNY. …Wow.

ALECK. …Yeah.

DANNY. You were serious?

ALECK. Were and am.

DANNY. That's one hell of a writer's block…from this building?

ALECK. From the top.

DANNY. Jesus…that's like…15 stories.

ALECK. 16.

DANNY. I read once that a penny falling from a hundred stories could kill a man.

ALECK. So?

DANNY. So I just hate to think what damage a man falling from 16 could do.

*(An awkward pause. **DANNY** smiles slightly, and after resisting it for several seconds, **ALECK** joins in the smile.)*

DANNY. So are we good?

ALECK. I suppose.

DANNY. Excellent. Now let's go over some ideas.

ALECK. Not tonight. Tonight I need to rest.

DANNY. Rest? I didn't talk you out of suicide so you could rest. If I knew you were going to rest, I wouldn't have argued.

*(Lights down. Short black out followed by lights up to reveal **ALECK** and **DANNY** in similar positions to their last.)*

DANNY. It's been three weeks.

ALECK. And four days.

DANNY. So?

ALECK. So.

DANNY. You know, God created the entire world in just six days. And you, Aleck, can't even come up with an idea in 25?

ALECK. Nope. So?

DANNY. So this better be one hell of a story with the time you're taking….let's brainstorm here. Themes? Morals? Shouldn't be too preachy. I don't want to read anything where a fluffy animal is going to tell me not to shoplift. But there should be some substance there.

ALECK. Right. Substance.

DANNY. I mean, cute is cute. But you're not cute.

ALECK. Really? And I thought you liked me, Danny.

DANNY. Eh. I like your creativity. But right now your creativity is losing big time to the fact that it's been three weeks and you still haven't had a single idea. I'm starting to think "The Suicide Note" by Aleck Chancey has the best shot of anything.

ALECK. Yeah, but I didn't have an ending.

DANNY. Sure, but the beginning was enthralling.

*(**DANNY** starts to chuckle. **ALECK** starts to laugh along, but stops when he sees **DANNY** staring him down, angrily.)*

ALECK. What?

DANNY. What's so funny?

ALECK. It's just that…that…oh, nevermind.

DANNY. I mean, I've been cutting you some slack because you say you're depressed. But then you start making jokes, cracking punch lines…being happy? I don't think so.

ALECK. Excuse me?

DANNY. Suicidal people cannot crack jokes. It doesn't work. If you're cracking jokes, you have no reason not to be writing.

ALECK. I see.

DANNY. Listen, Aleck.

ALECK. Yeah?

DANNY. Believe it or not, you're the third children's book author that I've had to talk down from suicide. Honestly. This is the third time I've had to talk a children's author out of suicide.

ALECK. Oh.

DANNY. And the second time I've been successful.

(pause)

And I've got to tell you, I'm getting tired of it.

ALECK. …Thanks.

DANNY. I'm tired of being here for you – being your handkerchief – and getting *nothing* in return.

ALECK. Well, I'm selfish like that.

DANNY. And being the kind-hearted *friend* that I am, I ask for no monetary reward for my concern. No monetary reward at all! Just a little favor. I ask you to *write something*. Which shouldn't be too demanding of a task, considering you're a writer.

ALECK. Shouldn't, but is!

DANNY. Exactly! Shouldn't, but is! So what's the problem?

ALECK. I've told you before what the reasons are.

DANNY. Oh, you have?

ALECK. Yes!

DANNY. And?

ALECK. I've got depression!

DANNY. Writer's block.

ALECK. Writer's block. Depression. Whatever.

DANNY. Fine. But that's not why you're not writing.

ALECK. I'm telling you, it is!

DANNY. Nuh uh. You just don't want to have to write.

ALECK. Why? What reason would I possibly have for wanting that?

DANNY. Because…because otherwise you have no reason to *say* you're depressed. No excuse. And that doesn't work for you. Because something inside you, something much more serious than writer's block, is keeping you from being happy, and you don't want to face it.

*(Long pause. **DANNY** recognizes that he has crossed the line. **ALECK**, at the same time, realizes that it's possible **DANNY** is right. **ALECK** slumps down on the couch and starts to think. **DANNY** is sorry, but he quickly regains his head-strong manner.)*

ALECK. I was a kid. Seven years old.

DANNY. Yes?

ALECK. First week of second grade. And I kept coming home from school crying because every other kid at Coppersfield Elementary knew the theme song to some junk kid's TV show, and I didn't.

DANNY. It's a cruel world.

ALECK. But it wasn't just that. I couldn't watch the TV show. I couldn't buy the toys that were advertised during the commercials of that TV show. Trampolines were too dangerous. Mountain Dew had too much sugar.

DANNY. What's the point?

ALECK. The point is, I didn't have a childhood! I had no childhood. Did you know I can't somersault?

DANNY. No, but I'm glad you told me.

ALECK. My parents never taught me that little kids were supposed to…that they were supposed to have fun… I didn't have a childhood.

DANNY. And I was born with flat feet. I'm Danny Brooks. You're Aleck Chancey. It's nice to meet you, I think you could write a children's book.

ALECK. How can I if I didn't have a childhood to draw upon? You're supposed to draw from your experiences when you write.

DANNY. I don't think Dr. Seuss was ever visited by a cat on rainy days, if it makes you feel better.

ALECK. No, but he knew what a rainy day was like for most kids. I didn't. I never did.

DANNY. Alright, so what do you want me to do? Teach you to somersault?

ALECK. I want you to help me, damn it! Look at me Danny, I'm a wreck. I'm 24 and I'm already balding.

DANNY. You're not balding.

ALECK. You're right. I'm shedding. And it doesn't end there. I can't sleep. I can't eat. I can't do anything. And I certainly can't write. I'm depressed, Danny.

DANNY. Lighten up, Aleck. You're always talking – crying – about how depressed you are. How miserable your life is. But why? Have you ever once given thought to what is *really* depressing about your life?

(pause)

What's really holding you back? You might want to think on it, Aleck. You might want to think very hard about what's stopping you from – from being you. Alright? So. My brother and his little girl are coming over tomorrow for dinner. I need an idea by then. They like you. They want to hear your stuff. Don't make Susie cry…again. Okay? Just one idea. Make me happy. Make yourself happy. One idea….

(DANNY *exits.* **ALECK** *walks over to desk, sits down at desk, begins to write, crumples piece of paper, lets out a short groan, and starts to write again.)*

ALECK. Dear Concerned Readers,

The blame for my untimely suicide does not fall on just one solitary person. Many people are at fault. First off, my parents for their injustices against me. You were the two that first put it into my head that…aw, screw it.

(ALECK reaches over to desk, opens a bottle of Advil, and pops several pills into his mouth. He sits down, and begins to reflect on the life he is now choosing to end. As a few seconds pass the lights should become more vibrant and colorful, suggesting something along the lines of a drug-produced high or trip. The pills ALECK have just taken start to produce a vision, and TEDDY, a product of ALECK's trip, walks out from behind the bookshelf, wearing a tightly buttoned trench coat with colorful clown-like clothes underneath. During the scene, after TEDDY has revealed his identity, the trench coat should fall open, revealing the clothes underneath.)

TEDDY. Trying to kill yourself again, Aleck?

ALECK. Who – Who are you?

TEDDY. Couldn't think of anything better than Advil?

ALECK. I'm afraid of heights.

TEDDY. That's a problem…Next time, however, you should try Sominex.

ALECK. Oh. Sominex.

TEDDY. Sominex works much quicker. The hallucinations aren't as *vivid*, though. When taking Sominex, you most certainly won't be visited by me.

ALECK. And who are you?

TEDDY. My name is Theodor S. Geisel.

ALECK. That name sounds familiar.

TEDDY. I was a writer.

ALECK. Anything I'd know?

TEDDY. After the relative failures of my first 13 books, I was thrown into a severe bout of depression.

ALECK. I swear I know that name.

TEDDY. I, too, tried to kill myself by overdosing on over-the-counter pills.

ALECK. It's *very* familiar.

TEDDY. However, I took only two more than the recommended dosage, and, as luck would have it, ended up tripping on the pills and seeing things rather than dying.

ALECK. I swear I know you.

TEDDY. During the aforementioned trip, I was inspired by my hallucinations and started writing what would become my first true hit. The book that catapulted me into stardom. Yep. Everything started to work out for me. After I wrote *How The Grinch Stole Christmas*, selling books was much easier, and I wasn't depressed…for a while.

(long pause)

ALECK. *How The Grinch Stole Christmas?* You're Dr. Seuss?

TEDDY. I was. Theodor Seuss Geisel…"Soice," actually, not Seuss. I could teach their children to love reading, but the parents still couldn't get my name right…assholes.

ALECK. YOU'RE Dr. Seuss?

TEDDY. What did you expect?

ALECK. Something…something more –

TEDDY. *(with constantly growing anger and contempt)* More? More what? More wob-tastic? More fanglerrific? You and everyone else. You want me to rhyme? You want me to be like my books? Like *Horton Hears A Who*? Make up silly words like my characters? I can do that. I can make up a damn word….Want me to try? Globbydoo. You know what it means? It means screw-you-and-all-you-damn-hypocrites-who-just-want-me-to-speak-in-rhyme-and-be-fun-for-the-kiddies-but-can't-stand-the-fact-that-I'm-a-druggie-who's-afraid-of-kittens-so-you-can-all-take-my-precious-books-and-shove-them-up-your-rumpledoodleoos…Not as fun as globbydoo, eh? No it's not. And I'm not the cat in the hat. I'm not Sam-I-Am…I'm Teddy Seuss *(pronounced "Soice" from here on by* **TEDDY***)* Geisel.

ALECK. I'm sorry. I didn't realize

TEDDY. What, that I have feelings? That the great Dr. Seuss may just be a little screwed-up up there? Yeah, you didn't realize. My readers didn't realize it either. They were happy and content sitting there reading *Oh, The Places You'll Go*...but if they knew the places that I was REALLY going, they wouldn't be smiling and laughing so. No one wants to hear about my problems. No one wants to hear anything I have to say that doesn't rhyme or make their children smile....

ALECK. It's a lot of pressure.

TEDDY. You're damn right it is. I don't know, maybe I could've been something more. Sometimes I'd wanna write about the war, maybe, and how it feels to be in the trenches watching your best friend die cause he's full of bullets, but then I'd remember I can't write about that because no parents want their children reading war stories.

ALECK. Were you in the war?

TEDDY. No, but I drew cartoons of it! It's really the same thing when push comes to shove. That's not the point. The point is sometimes I'd wanna write about my wife and her lovers, but children don't like reading stories about love affairs. And sometimes I'd wanna write about that insane passion I had to just one day end it all, put a stopper to all the stories and poems and my life (mostly my life), and just be at peace. But no one wanted to hear it.

ALECK. But you were successful, weren't you?

TEDDY. Success? What the hell is success?

ALECK. Well, you know. Selling books. Making money. That sort of thing.

TEDDY. If that's how you define success, you're screwed, kid. Success isn't some goal we have to reach. It's not some ribbon we can wear around our necks and flaunt. If that's what success was, I wouldn't be addicted to painkillers...No, success isn't the number of books you sell, or the number of women you...meet, or the dollars you make...It's all in your head, kid. You know the last time I felt really, *really* successful?

ALECK. No, I don't.

TEDDY. The last time I read a kid's book and really loved it. I was happy. I didn't care who wrote it, or if he was better than me. I was just content, sitting there, smiling...but that was before life screwed me over.

ALECK. I'm really sorry. Really, Dr. Seu-...Teddy.

TEDDY. Thanks. It means a lot. Sorry about that...outburst.... Do you mind if I smoke?

ALECK. Actually, I kind of –

(ALECK stops as he realizes that TEDDY has just taken out a bubble pipe, and is now blowing out bubbles, serenely. ALECK starts to speak. Stops. Looks at TEDDY, and shakes his head in resignation.)

No. Not at all. Feel free.

TEDDY. Thanks, kid. Now. Tell me, why did you want to write children's books in the first place?

ALECK. I don't know. I guess I knew I wanted to be a children's writer ever since I first learned to read. The books were my friends, cause I didn't have any real ones. And as I got older, I saw the joy that the books gave me on the faces of other children. So I guess that's why...I wanted to make kids smile.

TEDDY. How sweet. What about the children who can't smile?

ALECK. I'm sorry?

TEDDY. *(again, with escalating anger and contempt)* You heard me. The children who can't smile. I don't know. Maybe they're blind. Or they don't have a mom. Or they can't afford to go buy your books. Did you think about them? What about them?

ALECK. That's completely beside the point!

TEDDY. No. That *is* the point...Maybe you should have thought about them, and decided to become something else...an astronaut, or a farmer. Anyway...where was I? Right. I had just told you about how I wrote my books.

ALECK. ...*all* your books were the result of OD'ing on Advil?

TEDDY. No, no, no. Just the Grinch. I really preferred mushrooms.

ALECK. ....that's all they were? A druggie's rantings?

TEDDY. More or less. I was, however, sober when writing *One Fish Two Fish Red Fish Blue Fish*. But we saw where that got me.

ALECK. And you're here, appearing to me in a drug-induced vision....why?

TEDDY. Because you need to write. You need to face your fears, pick up a pencil, do some drugs, and write.

ALECK. This is insane. You chose me. Chose me and came to me to tell me to...take drugs, and to write?

TEDDY. Not just you. Any writer in need. Any writer desperate for a friend. Desperate for a muse. You. Eric Carle, writer of *The Very Hungry Caterpillar*. Maurice Sendak, *Where the Wild Things Are*. Dan Brown. J.K. Rowling... And see where I got them?

ALECK. All those authors? I refuse to believe that.

TEDDY. And not just them. Shakespeare. Ayn Rand...You remember the story *Goodnight, Moon*?

ALECK. Of course, that was one of my fav...Oh no. No. No. No. No.

TEDDY. *Goodnight, Moon* was nothing but a prolonged suicide note.

ALECK. No! How could you...? No!

TEDDY. It makes sense. Goodnight, Moon. Goodnight, chair.

ALECK. That's...that's horrible!

TEDDY. Goodnight, cow jumping over the moon. Seriously. Listen to the words. Goodnight, socks. Goodnight, clocks. Margaret Wise Brown was just saying, "Goodnight, life" ...I stopped her, though.

ALECK. Oh my god.

TEDDY. A good thing, too or else the last page's illustrations would have been a lot more morbid.

ALECK. You've just destroyed every reason why I ever wanted to be a children's writer.

TEDDY. Tough shit. This is the real world. And in the real world life can't be like our books. So I popped pills. So I did a few hits of acid. Look at the joy it gave children. I thought you wanted to see the children smile. Don't you want the children to be happy? You can make them happy. All you have to do…is take one more Advil…and you can start.

*(**ALECK** looks hesitantly at the bottle of pills.)*

ALECK. Will I be safe?

TEDDY. Hell, I'm a doctor, aren't I? *(pause)* Besides, you were just trying to kill yourself…Think about it.

*(**TEDDY** exits and **ALECK** picks up the Advil bottle. **ALECK** looks at the bottle, and sighs. Lights down. Lights back up on **DANNY** reading a manuscript as **ALECK** paces around very nervously.)*

DANNY. This is…good…And this is good…*This* is really, really good.

ALECK. You like?

DANNY. I like the idea. I like the characters. I think the talking furniture is cute.

ALECK. You like the story? You like the story.

DANNY. I love the story…What happened? Yesterday you couldn't even get an idea. Now you write one of the greatest children's stories I've ever read. What happened?

ALECK. …I tried to kill myself.

DANNY. Well, if it works….

ALECK. I'm not finished. I took Advil, a few more than I should have. And…I started seeing things.

DANNY. …what things?

ALECK. Well, Dr. Seuss – or…I guess…who I thought at the time to be (though it was really just the Advil, I guess) came to me and told me to do more drugs.

DANNY. I knew there was something fishy about him.

ALECK. Will you shut up for a minute? I'm being serious. Somehow. In my vision, he told me to do drugs, and then I could write a great story.

DANNY. So you did some drugs, and wrote *this*?

ALECK. No. *(pause)* No, I didn't. I walked over to the bookcase and picked up *The Very Hungry Caterpillar* and read it cover to cover. Then I picked up *The Lorax*. And I just kept getting more and more books. *If You Give a Moose a Muffin*. The *Frog and Toad* series. *Atlas Shrugged!* Every single one we own. And I read them all. And I was just happy, sitting there reading those books. Suddenly, I didn't give a damn about anything, I was going to be happy no matter what. Because I had friends, talent, and all the books I could ever need. So I just sat down, and wrote. And no matter what happens with this book, I feel pretty successful. I got it right, Danny.

DANNY. Whatever. You got it done. And it's good. I couldn't be happier...One question, though?

ALECK. Shoot.

DANNY. Who's this Teddy that you dedicated the book to? I thought *we* were best friends.

ALECK. We are, Danny, we are.

*(**DANNY** and **ALECK** exit. The stage is empty for several moments. **TEDDY** walks on, from behind the bookcase, and stops in front of it. He studies it for several moments, finds what he is looking for, and takes the book downstage and begins to read in a reminiscent tone.)*

TEDDY. *Oh, The Places You'll Go*, by...Dr. Seuss.

*(As **TEDDY** reads his book, he begins to realize the meaning of the words. He sees in the book all the dreams he once had. At times, he may giggle childishly at the optimism of the book. He stares off into the audience reflecting on the life he has led all wrong. He sighs, as he accepts his fate. **TEDDY** sadly closes the book, and places it on the desk as a reminder to **ALECK** of what success truly is. He walks, very slowly, past the bookshelf – and out the front door.)*

MECHANT ENFANT

by Samuel Mayer

CHARACTERS

ERICA, *a mother*
LOUISE, *her daughter*
BRANDON, *a friend of Louise*
FREDERICK, *a shopkeeper*

THE TIME

The present

THE PLACE

New York City

SYNOPSIS

A 7 year-old hangs herself in the nursery. Thus begins *Mechant Enfant*, which swirls around Brandon and Louise: two eight year-olds with a penchant for Tom Stoppard and Stravinsky. Together, along with the adults who they watch crumbling around them, they inhabit a gray, urban, privileged "tangle of nothingness". When in Mechant Enfant, a children's store, Brandon and Louise find both the solace they need and the all-too-real world of grown-ups they so desperately want. At turns funny, sinister, and poetic: *Mechant Enfant* is a startling, stylized, and grotesquely funny portrayal of childhood and survival.

MECHANT ENFANT was initially produced as a staged reading as part of the 2007 Young Playwrights Inc. (Artistic Director: Sheri Goldhirsch) Writers Conference Readings. It was held at Classic Stage Company and was directed by Linsay Firman. The production dramaturg was Joy Tomasko. and the stage manager for the reading was Annette Adamska. The cast was as follows:

ERICA . . . . Denise Bessette
LOUISE . . . . Marisa Viola
BRANDON . . . . Patrick Carlyle
FREDERICK . . . . Steven Hauck

(There are three playing spaces. When the lights come up:)

(A thin pair of legs hangs, suspended above the stage. Silence.)

(Footsteps are heard... Then a door opens, this is suggested only through lighting, a silhouette of a little boy looks upon the two legs, hanging from the ceiling. He pauses for a moment, looking at the pathetic little legs. Then, quietly, he shuts the door and the sound of him running down the hallway rings throughout the theater...)

(Left playing space. Lights up on a woman in her 40s. She is sitting on a lavish ottoman, in front of a lavish mirror, preparing to go out for the night. **LOUISE**, *her daughter – morose and wearing a frilly dress, sits on the floor, legs apart, gazing at a large pile of mail.* **ERICA** *talks to an unseen husband.)*

ERICA. *(as she powders her nose)* Richard, sometimes I think I'm just the luckiest woman in the whole wide world. I mean, here I am, look at me. Don't you think I'm just a VISION!? *(pause)* I think it's this lovely little thing you picked up for me at Carolina Herrera. I mean, REALLY Richard, it's just fabulously stunning. The whole shebang. And these diamonds, Ricky, oh my lord. I practically fainted the first time I put them on. So darling, really, and from Tokyo, too! They're so becoming on me.

LOUISE. *(calling to her mother)* Mother the mail!

ERICA. Yes dear. Yes.

LOUISE. *(to herself)* A&O Utilities... *(She opens the letter and takes out the bill.)* 600 dollars.

ERICA. *(dejectedly)* I don't like this eye shadow ONE BIT! *(pause)* Sometimes...Sometimes I think I'm just the ugliest girl in the whole wide world.

LOUISE. Conde Nast Publications...56 dollars.

ERICA. And I just cry myself to sleep... You hear me Richard, don't you?

LOUISE. *(examining a letter)* Mechant Enfant...478 dollars.

(There is a pause.)

Mother we're going to be late for play group. Mother! Mother?

ERICA. *(looking at herself in the mirror dejectedly)* One minute dear...One minute.

*(**LOUISE** looks at her watch. She stands up.)*

(blackout)

*(Central Park. Right space. **LOUISE** and **BRANDON**, dressed in a nice suit, stand.)*

LOUISE. Sorry about being late today. Mother isn't feeling well.

BRANDON. I understand. You'll send my condolences?

LOUISE. Of course I will.

(awkward pause)

LOUISE. *(smoothing out her frilly dress)* I picked up Channing Filch's new novel.

BRANDON. Oh? Really? How is it?

LOUISE. Delightfully droll. You know that I like Filch Brandon, I even liked *The Bird Cage Commeth*, which was a...

BRANDON. ...A masterpiece of dreck literature?

LOUISE. Well, that wasn't QUITE the turn of phrase I would've used, but, yes, I guess you could describe it thus.

BRANDON. What's the name of his latest? Something about a willow...right?

LOUISE. *A Weeping Willow Breathes Its Final Breath.*

BRANDON. And?

LOUISE. Ravishing. Simply his best.

BRANDON. No!?

LOUISE. Are you familiar with the premise?

BRANDON. I'm afraid not.

LOUISE. It's all about the death of a little girl in a small town, somewhere in Idaho, I think. How five citizens react, and what happens to them during a span of 48 hours.

BRANDON. Sounds like Irma LaCreme's 1968 novel, *A Passionate Affair in the Rivera*, except the scene has been changed to Idaho.

LOUISE. You see, that's the root of all the drama. There's nowhere to turn, no where to go. These poor Christ-fearing citizens find themselves captive to themselves, which eventually leads to their destruction, rebirth, or hideous downfall.

BRANDON. That's very interesting, in LaCreme's version, she has the four characters react differently to a murder, have you read it – ?

LOUISE. I have, and I must say, I find LaCreme's version to quite different than Filch's. After all, LaCreme focuses solely on a murder, and her story examines much more the price one pays for glamour, glitz and a decadent lifestyle. LaCreme's story is more of a "Rashomon", you know? While Filch tries to explain the human condition and the atmosphere of living in a small town. There's no anonymity in Podunk, Idaho. There's anonymity here. You get lost in the urban jungle. This jigsaw of buildings and that stench...

BRANDON. Five thirty.

LOUISE. Is it? Already?

BRANDON. I'll be seeing you?

LOUISE. Yes. I'll be seeing you.

(He exits.)

LOUISE. Death. That's it. Rotting, smelly, awful, putrid death.

(In the center playing area, two tiny wooden, stiff backed chairs have appeared. And sitting upon them is **LOUISE**

and **FREDERICK**, *a somewhat attractive 30-something who is the salesperson at* **Mechant Enfant**, *a high-end, Upper East Side children's boutique. The boutique is represented by a shelf of identical corduroy teddy bears that lines the entire span of the stage. The two sit drinking fake tea off a kiddie-tea-set. There is silence, then:)*

FREDERICK. *(jokingly)* I don't like this English Blend, do you?

LOUISE. Oh, I find it suitable for the mood that seems to have descended…

FREDERICK. What mood would that be, Louise?

*(***ERICA*** wanders through the pool of light, examining the merchandise. When she leaves:)*

LOUISE. *(thinking it over for a moment)* No. I don't like this blend, either. It's stale and has the fragrance of a horse.

*(***FREDERICK*** leans back in his chair…)*

FREDERICK. I've missed you, Louise.

(pause)

LOUISE. Yeah.

ERICA. *(wandering back on)* Louise, darling, ten minutes. Mommy says ten minutes.

LOUISE. *(when she's gone)* Mommy didn't know where the place was, Consuela quit last week.

FREDERICK. Did she?

LOUISE. *(leaning forward in her chair)* Yes. I woke up and I saw her leaving. She didn't see me though. Even though I said "goodbye." Mother actually picked me up from school today! I could hardly believe it when I saw her, but there she was! Smiling. 45 minutes late. But smiling. Of course she got lost on the way here.

FREDERICK. More tea?

LOUISE. I had peanut butter and jelly for lunch today. Mother didn't give me money to buy lunch.

FREDERICK. Has Brandon told you about his sister?

LOUISE. Monica? What about her?

FREDERICK. She's...Did you know Monica well?

LOUISE. Hardly. We'd met at social functions every now and then. Talent shows, parent night, you know.

FREDERICK. She hung herself.

(pause)

LOUISE. Oh?

FREDERICK. It's what I hear.

LOUISE. Do you know how?

FREDERICK. From a rope, I presume.

LOUISE. I see. That's... *(growing excited)* He's so lucky! That's straight out of Perry Mason...just think of it, Frederick. Real material for his novel!

ERICA. *(coming back)* Have you seen a salesperson, Louise, love? I can't seem to find one anywhere

LOUISE. *(getting up and stacking the tea cups)* This is him, Mother. Frederick.

ERICA. *(straightening herself out)* Oh, hello, sir! How do you do?

FREDERICK. I'm fine, madam. Did you find everything all right?

ERICA. You have such a darling little shop! It's simply enchanting!

FREDERICK. I'm so glad. Let's go to the register.

(The move to the stage right playing space.)

FREDERICK. $750, ma'am.

ERICA. It's my husband's card, is that all right?

FREDERICK. *(not missing a beat)* We don't study the names on the cards here, miss.

ERICA. *(laughing)* Good. Come now, Louise. Time to go.

FREDERICK. *(stopping them as they are exiting)* Louise tells me Consuela quit.

*(**ERICA** stops dead in her tracks.)*

ERICA. Did she? *(turning to **LOUISE**)* Louise...?

LOUISE. Yes, Mommy?

ERICA. Did you tell this man, this *stranger*, about Consuela?

LOUISE. He's not a stranger, Mommy. He's Frederick.

FREDERICK. – The only reason I asked was because, well, maybe, if you needed someone to look after Louise… you could, bring her here. I could…I could look after her just fine…It does get very lonely in here.

(**ERICA** *looks as if she's seen a ghost.*)

ERICA. *(curtly)* No thank you, that won't be necessary. Come Louise, you'll be late for violin. You know how Miss Primsini gets…

(*They exit…*)

(**BRANDON** *crosses the stage drinking something from a bottle in a brown paper sac.*)

(*As soon as he exits, lights up on the left playing area where* **ERICA** *sits, taking off her makeup for the day.*)

ERICA. Richard, darling, do you want to know something fantastic? *(pause)* Today, at Bulgari, Todd asked me if I'd like to try on some new bracelets he'd just gotten in and, it was then that I just thought to myself, you know, Erica, I don't. I DON'T WANT ANY MORE BRACELETS. *(pause)* That's not so bad, is it? Bracelets aren't everything, are they? There certainly are rings, dresses, earrings, necklaces…What's the deal with bracelets? I don't need any more, I have plenty. Don't you think? *(Pause. She drops her cold cream.)* Oh! You see, Richard, the other day It was rainy, so I had to cancel my hair appointment. Since I was staying in, I decided to go through the jewelry box, you know, weed out the unused gems. Anyway, I came across this little piece which I hadn't worn in years and I looked at it, and I said, "Why did I buy this?" What a waste of money! Anyway…I took Louise to this darling little place on Madison called…oh, what was it called…Mechant Enfant! *(drops creams)* How terribly French. I've no clue what it means, but doesn't the name just call out "darling darling darling"? *(pause)* Anyway, our little Louise goes there quite often and knows this salesman named...oh, what was his name? Never mind, I'll ask Louise. He seemed quite fond of her, you know. Quite fond...*(pause)* Richard. Are you listening? *(pause. nothing)* Richard. *(pause, thinking)* Did you hear what I said? Aren't you so proud of me? I'm being frugal, can't you tell? And then there are all these rings I have, have I shown you the one I picked up today at Tiffany's? You just have to see it. Let me...Oh now, where on earth did I put it? I swear I just had it...I swear...Oh Richard I – I...My lord – where is it!! *(She drops her cold cream again.)* Damn. *(She proceeds to wipe down her face and start reapplying the cold cream. She stops.)* Richard...? Have I already – ? *(She wipes her face again.)* Oh, never mind. *(pause)* I had to cancel lunch with Mrs Rockford tomorrow. You know her...Her son, Brandon, is Louise's friend. I just...You heard about her poor daughter, didn't you? I just don't think I could put on a brave face for her. You know how emotional I get at those "Planned Parenthood Lunches."

(ERICA picks up her cold cream, there's an envelope. She examines it.)

ERICA. *(calling to LOUISE)* Louise stop putting these idiotic bills in my bathroom! You've no idea the clutter it causes!

(ERICA gets up dramatically and moves to LOUISE, who's in the right playing space. She is sitting in a miniature armchair.)

ERICA. Did you hear what I said Louise?

LOUISE. Did you look at it, Mother?

ERICA. I haven't got time for this!

(ERICA collapses dramatically into an armchair identical to LOUISE's, just larger. Both are reading, now. ERICA is reading Vogue, *while LOUISE has her nose stuck into* Anna Karenina. *Silence.)*

ERICA. *(to* **LOUISE***)* What do you think of this dress? I think it's cute but the model positively ruins it!

*(***LOUISE*** is not amused. She doesn't look up.)*

LOUISE. It's very pretty, mother.

ERICA. *(pouty)* You didn't even look up.

(pause)

Would you ever wear fur, Louise? I think it's terribly tacky to these days. It used to be glamorous but it's just dangerous these days. You know, what with all those crazy NYU students who run around and throw paint on people's nice fur coats. But I think this one is just darling. *(shows her the picture)* How gorgeous, isn't it? Don't you think Louise? Would you wear that?

LOUISE. *(annoyed)* Yes mother.

ERICA. Girls your age shouldn't have furs, anyway.

(The telephone rings. **LOUISE** *answers it.* **BRANDON** *appears, holding another phone, in the left playing stage.)*

LOUISE. Hello?

BRANDON. May I speak to Louise please?

LOUISE. This is she.

BRANDON. Good evening, Louise. How are you?

LOUISE. I'm fine, Brandon. You're well, I hope?

BRANDON. *(coughing)* Ahem. Yes, yes, I'm excellent.

LOUISE. Good.

(pause)

BRANDON. *(simultaneously)* So, Louise… –

LOUISE. *(simultaneously)* Brandon… –

(They laugh nervously. Pause.)

BRANDON. Louise. I take it you heard about my sister?

LOUISE. Yes. I did.

BRANDON. Good. Well, that's why I'm calling, actually.

LOUISE. Oh?

BRANDON. Yes, I was wondering if you and your mother would like to join my mother and I at Bergdorf's after the funeral for tea, and my mother has tickets to the new Tom Stoppard play.

LOUISE. Might I ask how she got them? I've been trying for weeks!

BRANDON. Oh we've had them for months. My mother made sure to get us a box. We always have a box for Stoppard.

LOUISE. Well that sounds lovely, Brandon. Thank you.

BRANDON. *(relieved)* Good. I'll see you on Sunday at noon?

LOUISE. I think it will just be me, Brandon. You understand.

BRANDON. Of course.

LOUISE. Good.

BRANDON. Yes.

LOUISE. Well. Goodbye…

BRANDON. Goodbye.

(She hangs up and hops back into her armchair. Excited, book forgotten. **ERICA** *looks down at her)*

ERICA. Who was that?

LOUISE. *(not looking at her)* Brandon.

ERICA. Mrs Rockford's son?

LOUISE. Yes, Mother.

ERICA. Well, Louise. What did the boy want!?

LOUISE. Nothing mother. Nothing.

(She sits on her hands, excitedly. Rocking back and forth…)

ERICA. Very well, Louise. You're always so secretive.

(Left playing space, **BRANDON** *and* **FREDERICK** *appear, sitting at the little chairs.)*

BRANDON. Sometimes, Frederick, I think this is the only place in the whole word where I could ever be happy.

FREDERICK. *(leaning back)* Yeah?

BRANDON. All those teddy bears…

FREDERICK. *(pause)* They're pretty cuddly.

BRANDON. Outside of here, there's the street. There's all this commotion, there's this hectic world. But, one step inside your doors, and peace washes over you. It's so calming. It's so perfect. Everything down to the smell…*(He breathes in.)* Has Louise been here?

FREDERICK. Good job. She has.

BRANDON. *(proudly)* I could tell. Her nanny washes her hair with something that has coconut in it.

FREDERICK. Have you heard?

BRANDON. About Consuela?

FREDERICK. It travels!

BRANDON. I saw it coming. Louise told me she hadn't been paid in three months.

FREDERICK. She's a pretty little thing, isn't she?

BRANDON. Consuela? I never bothered to look.

FREDERICK. Louise, Brandon!

BRANDON. *(after a moment)* Yeah…yeah she is.

FREDERICK. You like Louise, don't you?

BRANDON. She's swell.

FREDERICK. Yeah.

(pause)

BRANDON. Do you remember my sister, Frederick? Monica?

*(There is a slight pause as **FREDERICK** considers what he knows.)*

FREDERICK. Of course. Nice little girl.

BRANDON. Right. Well. See. I…would you miss her if…she was sent to…Boarding School?

FREDERICK. Terribly. I'd miss her terribly.

(pause)

BRANDON. I should probably get going. Maria's probably sober enough to realize I'm not in the pram anymore…Might I trouble you for a balloon before I go?

FREDERICK. Of course.

(He goes and gets one.)

BRANDON. Thank you. Your balloon's always give me such comfort.

(pause)

Frederick? Do you think seven is too old to be wheeled through Central Park, across 79th, in a pram?

FREDERICK. Until you're ready to walk.

*(**BRANDON** gets up and holds out his hand for **FREDERICK** to shake. **FREDERICK** squats down to do so.)*

Always a pleasure.

*(He trots out, still holding his balloon, but forgetting his brown paper sack. **FREDERICK** goes over to it and takes out the bottle, taking out the straw first. It's coca-cola. **FREDERICK** starts to chuckle…)*

*(**ERICA** wanders in to Mechant, **FREDERICK** goes to her.)*

FREDERICK. I'm so sorry about the other day, ma'am. I was completely out of line –

ERICA. Oh no…! Please, think nothing of it.

FREDERICK. It was extremely poor taste of me to assume that you would want to leave your child with me, a stranger, like you so wisely said –

ERICA. Really –

FREDERICK. – Frederick.

ERICA. Really, Frederick. I thank you for wanting to help out. It's terribly noble of you. But, you see, there's absolutely no reason why we need you to help out. Everything's just fine!

FREDERICK. I see *(not seeing)*. Well then I applaud you, ma'am. For being in total control.

ERICA. *(laughing)* Oh really! You're just too much! Do you always speak like this?

FREDERICK. *(winking)* Only to the mothers. I'm sorry, I didn't catch your name –

ERICA. It's Erica. You can call me Erica.

FREDERICK. Nice to meet you Erica. Like I said, you'll remember that if you ever need any help with, Louise, you know, that sort of thing. I'm always here.

ERICA. Since Consuela left, we've had lots of bonding time. Me and Louise, I mean. I believe that I am finally beginning to understand this wonderful…thing, that I gave birth to. For years, I just thought of her as something to dress up, or to whip out at a dinner party to sing for friends, or to play the violin…She is much more. She is strong. A woman…something I never was. Something I'll never be. I looked over at her last night. At dinner, in between the salad and the roast beef, and she had tucked her napkin into her little dress. And it hit me… I thought, "My god. My daughter has TITS." She's already grown up. She's…she's…

(**ERICA** *collapses into one of the tiny chairs.* **FREDERICK** *doesn't know what to do. After a moment, he takes a teddy bear off the shelf, the change is jarring, and hands it to* **ERICA.** *She sobs into it.*)

I'm going to lose her before I even know her!

(**FREDERICK** *puts his hand on the woman's shoulder. She breathes heavily. After a moment. She takes his hand in hers.*)

Louise likes you so much. She talks about this place all the time.

FREDERICK. She does?

ERICA. You don't know…And it's so nice, really, it is. Louise loves it so much. And you're so great with the children. Like an angel…

FREDERICK. …thank you. I like Louise very much.

(*He holds her. There is a moment. He kisses her.*)

(**BRANDON** *is sitting at a wrought iron table in Central Park, central playing area. Holding his balloon.* **LOUISE** *enters, staring at him.* **BRANDON** *is looking for something…*)

BRANDON. I've lost my coca-cola, Louise. Have you seen it?

(**LOUISE** *gasps, thinking she was hidden.*)

LOUISE. Hello, Brandon.

BRANDON. It was in a brown sack. A little one.

LOUISE. Brandon, my shrink asked me why you aren't sad.

(**BRANDON** *stops looking and looks up at* **LOUISE.**)

BRANDON. Won't you have a seat?

(She does so.)

LOUISE. He says it's not normal for a boy not to feel grief.

BRANDON. Did he specify?

LOUISE. No, but I assume he meant "grief" in the sense of loss, emotional.

BRANDON. That would make sense, wouldn't it?

LOUISE. Why?

BRANDON. Why would that make sense?

LOUISE. No. Why don't you cry?

(pause)

BRANDON. I don't know…

LOUISE. That's not an answer Brandon.

BRANDON. Nothing inside me tells me that I should be crying. Plus, I'm much to excited to see the new Stoppard.

LOUISE. *(putting her head in her hands)* I don't understand Brandon! How can you even think about Tom Stoppard!

BRANDON. Maybe it's for the best that I do.

(She gets up to go. Pause.)

LOUISE. I'll see you Sunday?

BRANDON. Maybe at Mechant before then.

LOUISE. Perhaps.

BRANDON. "The Angry Child." What an odd name for a children's store. *(pause)* I've lost my coca-cola. Have you seen it?

(She sits back down.)

LOUISE. No, sorry.

BRANDON. I suppose Maria is looking for me. She always runs off

LOUISE. Is it important?

BRANDON. What?

LOUISE. The drink, Brandon.

BRANDON. Not particularly, but I'm not sure. Why don't you ask your shrink.

(pause.)

LOUISE. I'm sorry.

(nothing)

Are you mad that I told my shrink about your sister? Or is it because I told him you didn't cry?

BRANDON. I don't know…

LOUISE. *(getting up, suddenly enraged)* STOP SAYING THAT! It doesn't do anything! Stop running away from everything. From Maria, your mother, your fears…Your sister! Know something! Know anything!

BRANDON. My sister's dead.

LOUISE. No, Brandon!

BRANDON. She's GONE! GONE, LOUISE! What can I do!? WHAT CAN I SAY!? I don't even know what to feel! How do I know? What AM I feeling??

LOUISE. Didn't your heart give a little jump when you saw her there? Just hanging? Like a little pixie…A beautiful, dead, stockinged pixie…Did you not stop, just for moment, when you saw the marks that the rope made? Brandon…Please…show me you're alive…

(pause)

BRANDON. When I opened the door, and I saw her, I didn't even process it. I just went downstairs and saw Father reading the paper, and I saw Mother reading a magazine, and Maria was in her room, somewhere, doing something, and I just remembered something that happened, a long time ago, when we still lived on 65th. I had stubbed my toe and I was crying. And my mother came in, and said to me, "Brandon, love, quiet down. We're trying to read. Don't make such a fuss." So that's what I did. I didn't make a fuss. I went to play group and saw you and when I returned home...the body was gone.

LOUISE. *(in tears now, standing away from him)* But she's dead.

BRANDON. Not really, if you think about it. She's just left East 75th street. Maybe, if she's lucky, she's somewhere much hipper. The Village.

LOUISE. *(wiping her eyes)* Oh Brandon...

BRANDON. I still have every memory. I still have her smell. Her clothes. Her room, which Mother just painted blue...

And she's not gone, no. She's just...moved on, Louise. That's what she did. Moved on.

(He gets up to go to her, but he lets go of his balloon. He pauses momentarily, to watch it float out of sight...He moves to **LOUISE** *and hugs her. Comforting her.)*

Louise?

(quietly, after a moment:)

LOUISE. Yes?

BRANDON. *(softly)* My sister is dead.

*(***LOUISE** *turns around to face* **BRANDON.***)*

(barely a whisper:) Why'd she do it, Louise? Why?

*(***BRANDON** *sits back down. After a moment:)*

I've lost my balloon AND coca-cola. Great.

(He sniffs. Wiping his eyes, **LOUISE** *goes to him and sits down across from him)*

Why won't anyone listen to me?

LOUISE. Why won't anyone listen to any of us?
Sometimes I wonder what it's like off this Island.

BRANDON. The Bronx...?

LOUISE. There must be something beyond this tangle of nothingness. All this is is street after street after lonely street. And you wander it, and you live it, and you're all alone. Because what can you truly have, truly know, when all you see is leather bound books, cashmere sweaters and adults who smell depression and have twelve prozac in their mouths faster then you can say "postpartum"? It's like a backdrop in an old cartoon. Where Paris is nothing more than a whimsy sketch in pastels. Pink, green, lilac. Except, here, the colors are gray. Variations on a theme. A theme of solidarity, of this anonymous mass of people that move from point a to point b and don't see anything beyond their iPod. *(pause)* We all deserve to die, Brandon. Just like your poor sister. Because we can't sense grief or despair or sadness anymore. Because we feel it everyday. Because it's yours. Only, you've forgotten to feel it. Day after day...It's numbed you. What's emotion to a population that has no need for it? What's the point in bothering to speak when no one around you is ready to listen? When no one wants to listen? When no one wants to care. Or even accept. Here we stand. Trapped in shadows and not enough light hoping, praying, desperately that someone will listen.

(There is a moment of silence.)

Sometimes I wonder if everything we're taught is bullshit.

BRANDON. It would make us excellent novelists. *(pause)*

(There's a pause.)

Five thirty.

LOUISE. It always creeps up on us, doesn't it?

*(**ERICA** appears, right playing space, sitting at her mirror.)*

ERICA. Richard. Richard, I know this probably isn't a good time but...But, well, you see. We've been...evicted. Oh no! We're BEING evicted. We haven't been kicked out yet. The landlord, Mr Jefferson, says we haven't paid rent in almost four months. Were you aware of this? Why didn't you say anything, Richard? Darling, I know it's not a big deal, and I'll just dip into your account and pay the bill but, love, really, can't I rely on you to do the littlest thing? Like pay a bill?

BRANDON. Well I should find Maria. She's...

LOUISE. ...Probably done with her sailor.

(They stare at one another oddly. After a moment, BRANDON leans in and gives LOUISE a small kiss on the cheek.)

BRANDON. *(waiting)* Thank you.

LOUISE. For what?

BRANDON. For letting me –

LOUISE. *(cutting him off, uncomfortable)* Don't worry about it. It's not a big deal.

ERICA. But, I ask you, Richard, darling, please...Just a little money for my own allowance? The other day, the oddest thing happened. I was at Dean & Deluca buying these lovely looking strawberries and my card was...declined. Well, it's actually your card – but still! Declined! My lord, I was so embarrassed. So embarrassed. You have no idea, Richard. The way that everyone looked at me. I saw, I could tell. They all smiled at me but was soon as I'd turned my back – I heard their laughter. Mocking me. And Richard, you know winter's coming soon and I was thinking, perhaps it might be beneficial for me to have a fur coat. You know, something to keep me warm. I know it's not terribly fashionable these days but, really, Richard, when have I ever been concerned with what is and what isn't fashionable? Richard you've cut of my allowance. Aren't you going to say something. Give me an explanation! I think you owe me one. *(Pause. now holding back tears.)* Please. *(Pause)* Don't make me smear my mascara, Richard. Just say something. I love you? *(Pause, nothing. Now a croak:)* Richard!

*(Mechant. Center space. **FREDERICK** is arranging the merchandise. A bell rings, **LOUISE** has entered. **FREDERICK** turns around.)*

FREDERICK. *(cheerfully)* Hello Louise!

LOUISE. Is my mother here? Where's my mother?

*(**FREDERICK** falters a step, but not enough to be entirely noticeable.)*

FREDERICK. Hold up, you pretty-little-cupcake.

LOUISE. Frederick. I don't have any money. I just want to know where my mother is.

FREDERICK. *(He stops and faces her truly.)* I don't know, Louise. She was in her earlier today. But after that…I can't say. She was all jitters this morning.

LOUISE. *(moving to him, sitting in a little chair)* Frederick. I haven't seen her all day, she wasn't home this morning when I got up. I've called her cell and she didn't pick up. I've called everywhere! Her manicurist, nothing. All the galleries she goes to, nothing. her surgeon… nothing. And, Frederick, I promised Brandon I'd be at the funeral and help me put flowers on the grave. We're going to be late! It's almost eleven! Frederick, I'm worried.

*(**FREDERICK** sits down across from her.)*

FREDERICK. *(offering her same fake tea)* Tea?

LOUISE. Frederick!

*(**FREDERICK** sits the tea set back on the table. Silence.)*

Please, Frederick.

(after a moment:)

FREDERICK. She came in 'round nine this morning.

LOUISE. Nine? But that –

FREDERICK. When she's in the shop, she's very put together. Composed. Genteel. Not this morning. Her makeup was smeared, her hair was tangled, her clothes were messy, wrinkled. She kept on babbling on and on about her husband and this fur coat she wanted. This fur coat she just had to have. Louise, she wouldn't shut up. The only peace I got was when I kissed her.

(Pause as **LOUISE** *let's this sink in.)*

LOUISE. Kiss her?

FREDERICK. You remember what a kiss is? Don't you? Didn't you learn that in school?

(He leans in and gives her a kiss. There is an uncomfortable silence.)

Jogging your memory?

(nothing)

Let me try once again…This *(approaching her)* time on the *(centimeters away from her lips)*.

(As he kisses her, she slaps him hard across the face.)

Lips…

LOUISE. *(touching his cheek)* Frederick…

FREDERICK. Oh my god.

LOUISE. *(standing up)* Frederick…I…

FREDERICK. Oh my god…Oh my god.

LOUISE. I'm…I'm young, Frederick. I'm only 7, I'm just a little girl.

FREDERICK. You never seemed it. Never. I swear.

LOUISE. It doesn't matter what I *seemed* Frederick.

FREDERICK. Oh my god…

LOUISE. IT DOESN'T MATTER!

FREDERICK. Let me do it again, Louise. Please.

LOUISE. FREDERICK WHERE'S MY MOTHER!?

*(***LOUISE*** looks at ***FREDERICK*** pleadingly, desperately.)*

FREDERICK. *(growing frantic)* I don't know, I don't know… Louise stay, please.

*(***LOUISE*** looks at ***FREDERICK*** one last time.)*

Louise!

(She goes.)

(blackout)

*(**BRANDON** is seen in the left area, holding a black umbrella.)*

*(**ERICA** appears, center area, squatting on the ground. Mumbling to herself amidst fur coats and mannequins. **LOUISE** appears.)*

BRANDON. When someone is taken from our midst, what is the reason? What is the cause? What wicked thing have we done to invoke the wrath of such a terrible force that has the means to take a little eleven year old girl from 75th street? What did she do? She did nothing. The problem is she did nothing. She lived a life where she did not have a chance to stop. Somewhere between her GT elementary school, the art, drama, dance, poetry, volleyball, lacrosse, indoor soccer, swimming and SAT classes, something went wrong and because we all kept on going, we didn't turn back to notice that she'd fallen behind. And by the time we did, it was too late.

ERICA. *(groaning)* No…No…Stop coming at me…Stop…

LOUISE. Mother?

ERICA. Darling…Make them stop attacking me…All I wanted was a coat…A lovely fur coat…

*(**LOUISE** sees her mother and rushes to her, cradling her.)*

ERICA. Louise? Darling? Is that you? The models, love… the models…they're saying things. Mean things.

LOUISE. Mother. Please.

BRANDON. What is a child without a childhood?

ERICA. Why are they coming at me? Get Richard…Get Daddy…call him…

LOUISE. I can't, Mother

ERICA. Why? I want him so

LOUISE. Richard left, Mother. Daddy left a year ago.

(There's a pause.)

BRANDON. I'm sorry, dear Sister. I didn't mean to lose track of you it's just…there's always so much to be done. So I am the first to watch you be lowered into the cold earth, and I pray that wherever you are, there is something better. Something realer.

ERICA. Gone Louise?

LOUISE. Gone.

ERICA. Louise, I don't understand.

LOUISE. I don't either.

Give me that.

(She takes a bottle of pills from her mother's clutches.)

BRANDON. When I was three years old, and was learning to read, my parents bought me a book called *Baby Sartre in the Palace of Charlamagne*. When I was four years old, I wrote a poem for *The New Yorker*. When I was five I was the best speller in the city of New York.

LOUISE. We have to go, Mother.

ERICA. But the coat…

LOUISE. We can't buy the coat, Mother.

BRANDON. I've never had a snowball fight, before.

ERICA. *(looking up, with surprising clarity)* Louise?

*(**LOUISE**, startled, stops.)*

I love you.

(pause)

LOUISE. Yes, Mother. Yes.

(Their area goes dark.)

BRANDON. Good bye. I'm sorry. I'm so sorry.

(His area goes dark.)

(Darkness. It's calm. Some time has passed.)

*(**LOUISE** and **BRANDON** appear in the center playing space.)*

LOUISE. I'm sorry we missed the Tom Stoppard.

(pause)

BRANDON. It got bad notices.

LOUISE. I think it's for the best.

(pause)

BRANDON. Yes. Yes, I think so.

(pause)

So you're leaving?

LOUISE. We have to.

BRANDON. Where are you going?

LOUISE. Indiana.

BRANDON. Christ.

LOUISE. Yeah, that's what I said…But it won't be so bad. In fact – I'm almost looking forward to it. In a weird way.

BRANDON. A really weird way.

LOUISE. I think there's a time when you have to know "that's it." And, well, "this is it."

BRANDON. All the luck in the world, Louise.

LOUISE. Thank you. I'll be back.

BRANDON. I hope so. I'll miss you. And visiting the park. And the store.

LOUISE. And Frederick.

BRANDON. *(agreeing)* and Frederick.

(content pause)

*(Although **LOUISE** does not go to him, **FREDERICK** appears, and they talk.)*

FREDERICK. You're leaving. I didn't know.

LOUISE. Goodbye Frederick.

FREDERICK. I love you.

LOUISE. No, you don't.

FREDERICK. I do, Louise. I do very much.

LOUISE. Let's part on good terms.

FREDERICK. Come back and see me?

*(**ERICA** appears in the last remaining pool of light, she's dressed for traveling and is accompanied by many bags.)*

ERICA. Louise! Louise let's go!

LOUISE. Of course, Frederick.

(to **BRANDON***:)* I brought you this book.

(She produces a thin paperback.)

BRANDON. *(reading the title)* A Weeping Willow Breathes Its Final Breath. By Channing Filch. Thank you.

LOUISE. Read the last page.

(He opens the book and reads it.)

ERICA. LOUISE! WE'RE GOING TO MISS OUR FLIGHT!

BRANDON. "Every time the sun rises, the sun sets. Every time the moon rises, the moon sets. The sun, the moon, they are forever. A willow...A willow weeps until its tears are gone. Than a willow dies. And when a willow dies. It is ready. A willow does not go down alone and unprepared. A willow is strong. A willow is aware and when a willow takes its final breath, the whole world shakes."

*(***LOUISE*** slowly walks over to* **FREDERICK** *and gives him a kiss on the cheek.)*

(blackout)

End

THE METRONOME

By Gabriel Neustadt

CHARACTERS

JAKE FORD - late twenties/early thirties, piano instructor
DOUGLAS GERSHOM - elderly

SYNOPSIS

An old man must come to terms with his misspent life and ensuing death; his young piano instructor is in danger of taking the same path. A conversation between the two leads to an understanding of who they are and the choice one of them must make.

SCENE: DOUGLAS'S HOME / LIVINGROOM / DAY

(Lights rise. A piano sits in the corner of the room. **DOUGLAS** *waters what appears to be a dead potted plant. Doorbell rings.)*

DOUGLAS. Come in! The door's unlocked!

(Enter **JAKE**. **DOUGLAS** *talks with an intelligent air.)*

JAKE. Mr. Gershom!

(They shake hands.)

DOUGLAS. You know I go by Douglas, Jake –

JAKE. Douglas.

DOUGLAS. And "Jake" – such a beautiful name. You should be so proud of your name. Means "supplanter," no?

JAKE. Uh – yeah, I think so. Never considered it "beautiful."

DOUGLAS. Very. Very beautiful meaning, too: "supplanter." It's really so fascinating – the meanings of names and all.

(beat)

JAKE. So how are you today, Douglas?

DOUGLAS. Good! Any time you wake up above ground, it's a wonderful feeling.

*(***JAKE*** politely smiles.)*

DOUGLAS. How are you?

JAKE. Oh, I'm all right. Better than that.

*(***DOUGLAS*** laughs.* **JAKE** *is pointing at* **DOUGLAS'** *plant.)*

Every time I come here, that plant looks worse and worse. Do you want me to throw it out for you? –

DOUGLAS. No, it'll grow; I'm not going to give up on it yet.

JAKE. Well, that type of plant should really be kept in full sunlight, and it looks like you're watering it too much.

DOUGLAS. I didn't know you had a green thumb, Jake! –

JAKE. I'm not really, I just –

DOUGLAS. Why don't you take it? Maybe you can make it grow.

JAKE. Oh, no, I better not –

DOUGLAS. No, take it.

JAKE. I'll think about it.

DOUGLAS. Alright.

(new subject)

Yes, Rose gave it to me on our 50th anniversary. She's been in the kitchen all day baking friendship bread for the neighbors.

JAKE. *(beat)* Oh, how nice.

DOUGLAS. It takes ten days to make – to rise and all that. Goodness, she's probably been making it for the last sixty years!

JAKE. Wow, that's really something.

DOUGLAS. Yes. Very sweet tasting. It has apple in it. Walnuts. Figs.

JAKE. Mmmm.

DOUGLAS. I know she's made some for you before.

JAKE. Um, yeah, it was very good.

(beat)

JAKE. So, recital tomorrow –

DOUGLAS. Recital?

JAKE. Yeah, remember? You're playing –

DOUGLAS. Oh, that's right! How could I forget? I'm very excited.

JAKE. Do you think you'll be ready?

DOUGLAS. I hope so!

JAKE. Well, let's find out.

DOUGLAS. In a moment. Something to drink?

JAKE. No, no, no – don't get up – I'm fine.

DOUGLAS. No, please, I would be delighted.

JAKE. No, really, I'm fine.

DOUGLAS. Alright.

(beat)

So have you thought any more about the Bard fellowship?

JAKE. No – I haven't had much time lately. Just trying to be practical for now –

DOUGLAS. Oh.

*(He gives **JAKE** some magazine clippings.)*

DOUGLAS. I did some research on it, and I found out that Melvin Chen and Richard Goode teach there.

JAKE. I'm not familiar with them.

DOUGLAS. Apparently, they're very famous. Julliard, Carnegie Hall, you know. When you graduate, you'll be a world-class concert pianist!

JAKE. Oh, wow…I'm actually in a bit of time crunch, so if we could, I'd like to start as soon as possible.

DOUGLAS. Alright, that's fine. How about now?

JAKE. That would be wonderful, thank you.

*(With **JAKE**'s assistance, **DOUGLAS** hobbles to the piano, his withered arthritic limbs under paper-thin skin straining under his slight frame.)*

DOUGLAS. Thank you.

JAKE. You're very welcome.

DOUGLAS. You know what I just noticed.

JAKE. What?

DOUGLAS. We both have the same carriage. We both hold ourselves the same way, with the shoulders and all? Did you notice that?

JAKE. No.

DOUGLAS. Really? Almost exactly the same. It's really remarkable how similar we are to each other, Jake.

JAKE. I don't see any resemblance.

DOUGLAS. Oh, you must. You look just like I did when I was your age: same hair color, shape size – let me show you some pictures –

JAKE. Don't get up, it's fine. How about we look at the end of the lesson? –

DOUGLAS. Alright. But even personalities when I was your age. Cool, quiet, conservative. But still interested in the world a little, no?

JAKE. Maybe. What should we start out with today? Hannon to warm up?

DOUGLAS. First –

JAKE. Number 2. Remember what we discussed last week about keeping the rhythm steady. Tat tat tat tat tat tat tat tat. Do you want me to time you yet?

DOUGLAS. Um, no, not yet.

JAKE. Alright. Let's see how you did.

DOUGLAS. OK.

(**DOUGLAS** *begins the exercise, weakly and slowly tapping out each note, failing to keep time. He struggles and stops after a few measures.*)

JAKE. *(while **DOUGLAS** plays)* Try to keep time. Nope, that's an E. E. A. Dee da dee dee dee dee dee da *dee* da dee dee dee dee dee da *dee* da *dee*...

(etc.)

DOUGLAS. *(laughing)* Well, it certainly sounded better during practice!

JAKE. That's fine. How 'bout we warm up on something else?

DOUGLAS. First: warm up our minds. That was always something my father told me to do. "Warm up you mind before you do anything, Douglas." See, I almost forgot: Monday was the 440th anniversary of the Spanish landing in St. Augustine.

JAKE. Wow, I never knew that.

DOUGLAS. Yes, well I thought since you were a history major, you'd find it interesting.

JAKE. I was a music major.

DOUGLAS. Right, right. Yes, that's right. But 440 years ago! On Monday! Goodness, that's almost as old as I am!

(He chuckles. **JAKE** *smiles politely.)*

DOUGLAS. Yes, see, when you get to be my age, Jake, you start to think in decades, not months.

JAKE. Like the Chinese?

DOUGLAS. No, the Chinese say they think in *centuries*, Jake.

JAKE. Centuries!

DOUGLAS. Centuries. But I can't count that high, Jake, I'm a lawyer. I can only think in decades now. But here's a perfect example: if Bush had just thought in decades and remembered what his father had known about removing Hussein, we never would have gotten into this mess.

JAKE. Well, I can't say I disagree with that.

DOUGLAS. Very good. God, what a mess. I was reading the *New York Times* this morning – I know you get the *Times*.

JAKE. I have an online subscription –

DOUGLAS. Very good – I don't understand all this technology – but anyway, I was reading in the *Times* this morning this editorial written by four sergeants in Iraq – did you see that?

JAKE. I saw it, and I was going to read it, but I had to go –

DOUGLAS. I highly recommend you read it. You *must* read it as soon as you get the chance, Jake. It certainly puts a different perspective on the war. It was in response to that O'Hanlon/Pollack piece from a few weeks ago. Very interesting. I'd like to hear what you have to say about it when you get the chance to read it.

JAKE. Well, I'll definitely try to read it.

DOUGLAS. I'm looking forward to discussing it with you.

JAKE. Same. But let's try the Hanon again. I brought a metronome with me. It might help.

DOUGLAS. Oh, Jake, I think my hands might be getting a little bit tired of Hanon!

JAKE. Alright. Did you get to practice that C scale?

(He turns on the electronic metronome.)

DOUGLAS. *(talking over the metronome)* A little bit.

JAKE. That's good. And there are only twelve major scales, so you're already, what, eight per-cent of the way there?

DOUGLAS. *(hurt)* I didn't know you're a mathematician too, Jake! So talented! Music, history, math. I bet you're a scientist, too. I always wanted to be a scientist. I remember always reading about the Manhattan Project in the newspapers – very secretive. If you ever wanted to get through to a call quickly, you would say to the operator, "It's about the Manhattan Project," and she would say, "Right away!" –

JAKE. Interesting. Just begin when you're ready.

DOUGLAS. *(nervously)* Which note do I start on?

JAKE. C to C, remember? Look for the two black keys. Underneath the letters. That's right. Start when you're ready.

*(**DOUGLAS** plays poorly, messing up his fingering and resorting to tapping the keys with his index fingers. **JAKE** has to slow the metronome to match **DOUGLAS**'s slow pace. **DOUGLAS** finishes his simple scale. It was terrible. The metronome continues to play.)*

JAKE. It's easy once you get the pattern going.

DOUGLAS. Yes, I suppose so. I changed parties, you know.

JAKE. I'm sorry?

DOUGLAS. I never told you I switched parties?

JAKE. What – political parties?

DOUGLAS. Absolutely. First Democrat ever in my family. You see, Jake, we come from a *long* line of Massachusetts Republicans.

JAKE. *(smiling)* Oh, I see. What caused you to do it?

DOUGLAS. Principles, like anything. The party left me. They've gotten so terrible: neglecting the poor, neglecting the elderly. Xenophobic – that metronome's driving me crazy – I don't know how you can stand it –

JAKE. Sorry –

DOUGLAS. Diplomatically irresponsible. Fiscally irresponsible. They've gotten so anti-tax while they've spent so much – I don't understand how anyone can still support them. It's awful. They've forgotten that taxes are your *duty to society*. My point is, it's never too late to change. Political parties, anything.

JAKE. You're absolutely right.

DOUGLAS. And if I were younger, I'd run for Congress right now to change it, though my family would be rolling in their graves if they knew I was running as a Democrat.

(He laughs. JAKE laughs politely.)

DOUGLAS. But I guess that's what you'll have to do, Jake. No?

JAKE. What?

DOUGLAS. Run for Congress! Senator Jake Ford – I could hear myself calling you that. I'd have to work for your campaign, though, wouldn't I? Licking envelopes, maybe?

JAKE. *(laughs)* Yeah, sure.

DOUGLAS. You would make a fine senator, Senator Ford. Though you'd have to get a law degree first, I suppose. But whatever you do, don't become a lawyer. Don't play it safe. Do something you love.

JAKE. What if I love arguing?

DOUGLAS. Then get married. I hope Rose didn't hear that!

(mimics Rose)

"Douglas! I don't hear any music!"

(He laughs. JAKE smiles.)

DOUGLAS. But I know *you* love music. You're destined for greatness.

JAKE. That's not what really happens to people –

DOUGLAS. Oh, don't kid me, Jake. You're not going to be some nobody. That's why you're going to apply for the fellowship, no? $15,000 yearly stipend –

JAKE. *(hurried)* Right. Let's start your recital piece for tomorrow.

DOUGLAS. You *are* going to –

(**JAKE** *opens* **DOUGLAS**'s *beginning level book for piano.*)

JAKE. *(checking his watch)* Let's focus on tomorrow, alright?

(Pause. **JAKE** *shifts uncomfortably.)*

DOUGLAS. Who else would be playing at this recital?

JAKE. There'll be students from programs all over the county, Douglas, we've already gone over this.

DOUGLAS. And is this a recital for beginners?

JAKE. No, well, the beginners play first –

DOUGLAS. I'm with the beginners? –

JAKE. Yeah. So – so then there'll be an intermission before the advanced kids –

DOUGLAS. Will there be any adults playing?

JAKE. Oh, I don't know. Usually not.

DOUGLAS. So it'll just be children –

JAKE. Probably.

(uncomfortable pause)

DOUGLAS. Yes…so…perhaps this isn't the recital for me, Jake. If it's just going to be me with a bunch of *(laughs)* children…Let's talk about your fellowship –

JAKE. "Twinkle, Twinkle Little Star." Let's play that now.

(pause)

DOUGLAS. OK! "Twinkle!" Mozart! Did you know he wrote it when he was five –

JAKE. That's a common misconception – he wrote a variation on the melody later in life.

DOUGLAS. Oh –

JAKE. Just begin when you're ready.

(Pause. Hunched over, **DOUGLAS** *tries to play. In a protracted attempt, clumsily and without rhythm, he tries to tap out the song with his index fingers. His hands shake. This takes a good deal of time.)*

DOUGLAS. Damn, I lost my place.

JAKE. Remember, you're right here.

(He hums the melody.)

DOUGLAS. I was?

JAKE. Yes.

*(**DOUGLAS** keeps trying, pathetically tapping out the song. **JAKE** sets the metronome on 116 bpm. **DOUGLAS** cannot keep up. **JAKE** slows the metronome to 92 bpm. Still, **DOUGLAS** cannot keep up, his hands shaking. The slowing metronome sounds like a heart monitor of a dying man.)*

(72 bpm.)

(56 bpm.)

(46.)

(44.)

(42.)

(40.)

(Tick...Tick...Tick...Tick.... –)

*(Beeeeeeeeeeeeeeeee...The tuning note sounds like the stopped-heart sound on a heart monitor. [**JAKE** has accidentally turned the metronome past its slowest setting.] Pause as the siren continues to play. **JAKE** shuts off the metronome. Pause.)*

JAKE. *(while **DOUGLAS** fidgets with the dead plant)* Douglas, you obviously haven't been practicing. I haven't seen any improvement since we started these lessons. The only way we can make this work is if you do what I assign you each week. If it's too much, please tell me, and I'll cut back.

DOUGLAS. No, it's not that –

JAKE. Then what is it? How do you ever expect to get better? How do you expect to learn anything if you can't play in front of some kids?

DOUGLAS. I –

JAKE. *(intensely)* Mr. Gershom, you're not being *practical*. We both have to put in effort if you want to learn how to play.

DOUGLAS. Jeff –

JAKE. Mr. Gershom, you have to keep moving. You have to focus. *Focus.* You gotta quit stopping to smell the flowers and do what you gotta get done, do you understand me? And if you want to play in tomorrow's recital –

DOUGLAS. I don't want to play in tomorrow's recital.

JAKE. Yes you do –

DOUGLAS. I never did, Jack –

JAKE. And my name is *Jake*.

(pause)

DOUGLAS. I know Rose doesn't agree with your philosophy, Jeff. We were talking about you recently –

JAKE. Really? –

DOUGLAS. Yes, Rose was saying how she thought you were almost too…pragmatic. Very pragmatic. I bet you have a schedule for everything, Jake, don't you? Have you planned when you'll be watching television tonight? Or what you're going to eat for breakfast tomorrow?

(He laughs.)

See, Jake, I think you *do* need to smell the roses once in a while. You have to seize all your opportunities, or you may end up like me! An old, boring man! You don't want to be a *fail*ure –

JAKE. And what's a failure? –

DOUGLAS. An old, boring man, Jake, that's a failure.

JAKE. Well, I wholeheartedly disagree.

DOUGLAS. Wholeheartedly?

JAKE. 100%. A failure is someone who wastes his time chasing goals he has no chance of meeting.

DOUGLAS. You're completely wrong. A failure is anyone who doesn't do what he *knows* he should do, Jake.

(He laughs.)

DOUGLAS. *(cont.)* That's what Rose said, and Rose is a very smart woman.

JAKE. Douglas, I've never seen Rose.

(beat)

DOUGLAS. That's ridiculous! She made you friendship bread.

JAKE. I'm afraid you were confused. She's never made me friendship bread. I've never seen her.

DOUGLAS. She's been in the kitchen.

JAKE. I've never seen her.

DOUGLAS. She's been right in the kitchen.

(beat)

JAKE. Mr. Gershom, could you go into the kitchen and bring her out to see me?

DOUGLAS. Yes, she's right in the kitchen.

*(Pause. **DOUGLAS** touches the dead plant.)*

JAKE. I'd like to say hi to her, Douglas.

DOUGLAS. Oh yes. Absolutely.

JAKE. *(calling to the kitchen)* Good afternoon, Mrs. Gershom! –

DOUGLAS. You know she prefers you call her Rose.

JAKE. Good afternoon, Rose! How are you doing today? I'd like to see you! Can you come out for a second?

(pause)

JAKE. Mr. Gershom, I don't think Rose is in the kitchen –

DOUGLAS. What? That's nonsense.

JAKE. Think, when was the last time you saw her?

*(Pause. **DOUGLAS** has a confused look on his face.)*

JAKE. Wait – …

*(**JAKE** looks horrified at himself.)*

*(**DOUGLAS**' expression shifts to a very worried look [**DOUGLAS**: maybe she is dead!])*

DOUGLAS. *(snapping out of it)* She just left for the store.

(Long pause. **DOUGLAS** *again fidgets with the dead plant.)*

JAKE. I can't – I really don't see any point to continue these lessons. I mean, what's the point of having these if we don't get anywhere?

(long pause)

DOUGLAS. Will you just talk with me, please?

JAKE. I'm sorry?

DOUGLAS. Talk with me. Sit down and talk with me about things, Jake.

(beat)

DOUGLAS. Why do you think I take these lessons? To play in some recital with six year-olds?

(pause)

I take lessons from you, Jake, because I enjoy your company. This is the highlight of my week. What else is there to look forward to? Now I'm dying and this is it? I haven't done anything yet, Jake. I've lived a safe, average, decent life. You'll hate yourself for it.

This could be your last chance, Jake. You *must* apply for the fellowship! You *must* apply –

JAKE. You think a few words of advice from you or anyone else can change the course of my life? I'm not good enough, Douglas. There were 12 keyboardists in my undergrad program, and I was 10th best. I'm not a great pianist!

(pause)

DOUGLAS. I know. But it's no reason to give up. You don't have much time to do something with yourself, Jake, at least try.

(pause)

DOUGLAS. You're scared to death.

JAKE. So are you.

(pause)

DOUGLAS. You're right. I am. I've traveled the path of mediocrity. Convincing you not to is all I can do.

(long pause as they each think)

DOUGLAS. I suppose the lesson's over.

JAKE. Uh, yeah – I better get going.

(He moves to exit.)

DOUGLAS. Lesson next week?

JAKE. Um, yes, of course.

*(**DOUGLAS** motions to the withered plant.)*

DOUGLAS. *(beat)* Will you take this?

JAKE. *(pause)* Sure.

*(Pause. **JAKE** takes the potted plant from **DOUGLAS** and moves to exit. Pause. Fade out with **JAKE** at the door as the two look at each other.)*

End

UNWANTED ADVENTURE

By Brandon Johnson

CHARACTERS

- **BETH** - A typical teenage girl, desperately wants to go to sleep. Senior in high school. Very sarcastic at times.
- **MR. NARRATOR** - Never seen, but an older man, maybe in his 40s. Always gets his way. Very cocky and bossy. His voice is similar to the announcer on the show *Superfriends*.
- **CARL** - An evil super genius bad guy who lacks common sense. He is geeky, overweight, and short tempered. Lives in his mother's basement (a.k.a. The Carl Cave).
- **GUYS IN BLACK CLOTHING** - They move the set and do whatever Mr. Narrator asks them to. Lots of unnecessary arm movements.
- **CARL'S MOM** - Never seen. Late 70s, loves to spoil her little Carl. Enjoys long walks on the beach, candlelit dinners, and that feeling of freshness when she puts in her dentures after they have been brushed.
- **SHOW GIRLS** - Ever see the those game shows where they have the glamorous girls showing off the cool prizes you can win and have those really fake smiles? Yep, those are these gals.
- **FAT GUY** - Preferably not actually large, and just some stuffing in his shirt. He is just a model of what the world is to become. Very clumsy.

SYNOPSIS

After a tiring day, all Beth wants to do is go to sleep, but unfortunately for her, she can't. Due to a case of mistaken identity, she gets roped into saving the world from a middle aged geek who lives in his mothers basement using the internet to hypnotize people. The only thing Beth has to help her is a mysterious voice who goes by the name of Mr. Narrator. Beth thinks everything going on is bogus, but if it will help her get to bed sooner, she'll do whatever it takes. Will Beth have the right stuff to save the world so she can get back to her bed?

COSTUMES

BETH - PJs, bunny slippers, two ponytails.

MR. NARRATOR - Never seen, so it doesn't matter. He could be naked if he wanted to be.

CARL - Gaming shirt, glasses.

GUYS IN BLACK CLOTHING - Black clothing (go figure) preferably leotards, or anything extremely embarrassing, just for added humor.

CARL'S MOM - Same as Mr. Narrator.

SHOW GIRLS - Glitzy dresses that shine in the light.

FAT GUY - Regular plain clothes should suffice.

PREVIOUS PRODUCTION

CAST

BETH	Hillary Hoyt
MR. NARRATOR	Christian Clapp
CARL	Nik Frazee
GUYS IN BLACK CLOTHING	Brittany Heath
	Tim French
	Kim Poulette
	Shawnnee Johnson
	Marion Nickerson
CARL'S MOM	Brittany Heath
SHOWGIRLS	Shawnee Johnson
	Brittany Heath
FAT GUY	Tim French

CREW

Director - Brandon Johnson

Lights/Sound - Alex Webster

Scene 1: BETH'S ROOM

(BETH is in her room wearing PJs and is talking to her friend Sarah on her cell phone. There is a twin-sized bed upstage center, and a bed stand with a digital alarm clock showing 11:00 PM and a lamp turned on to the right of it. There is a small computer desk or table upstage right.)

(BETH is pacing back and forth while talking on her cell phone.)

BETH. *(on cell phone)* That Janie is such a slut! How dare she do that with Devin, I mean it's only been two days since you two broke up. *(listens to SARAH for a moment)* I know! *(checks clock on bed stand)* Well, we'll discuss this more tomorrow. Right now, I gotta get to bed. I'm exhausted from basketball practice. Bye Sarah. *(She hangs up phone, yawns, gets into bed, shuts off lamp, and closes eyes to sleep.)*

MR. NARRATOR. *(loudly, offstage into a microphone in an announcer like voice)* We find our hero snoozing in her bed, unaware of what is about to happen.

BETH. *(turns on lamp quickly, frightened)* Who's there?

MR. NARRATOR. Suzanne was about to be assigned a dangerous mission to save the planet!

BETH. *(scared to death that somebody may have broken in to her house)* Where are you? Who are you? *(pause, then confused)* Who the hell is Suzanne?

MR. NARRATOR. *(chuckling)* Silly girl, I am everywhere, you should know that by now! I am Mr. Narrator, your boss, your master! As for that last question, which is the dumbest of all, you are! Honestly, who doesn't remember their own name? Anyway, do you accept your mission to save the world?

BETH. *(getting control of herself, but still bewildered)* I don't know where you're getting your info, but I've never known you, and my name is certainly not Suzanne. It's not even close. It's Beth.

MR. NARRATOR. Come again?

BETH. You heard me, I'm not Suzanne. You have the wrong person.

MR. NARRATOR. *(embarrassed by his mistake)* Oh. I see. Could you by any chance, um, tell me where she lives?

BETH. *(angry)* Sorry dude, I can't help you. Now, if you would excuse me, get the hell out of my house before I call the cops. I'd like to get back to sleep. *(starts to lie back down)*

MR. NARRATOR. There is no time! I don't have enough time to get to the *(mockingly)* REAL hero's house. You'll have to take her place.

BETH. *(irritated)* No! Leave me alone!

MR. NARRATOR. Please! The fate of the world is in your hands!

BETH. *(getting extremely aggravated)* NO!

MR. NARRATOR. *(sounding desperate)* But you must! *(pause, then quietly)* Please?

BETH. *(in a temper)* FINE! If it will make you leave me alone. *(to self)* I must be going crazy or something.

MR. NARRATOR. Splendid! You'll have to begin some fast track training right away, Barb. Check under your bed, there is a duffel bag with training gear.

BETH. Whatever. And the name is Beth*!*

(Gets out of bed, aggravated, and finds the duffel bag and opens it. She finds a jar of unopened pickles, a Rubik's cube with one turn left to solve it, and a teddy bear. **BETH** *places each item beside each other on the desk and says each item as she takes it out.)*

An unopened jar of pickles, an almost completed Rubik's cube, and…a teddy bear? Is this some kind of sick joke?

MR. NARRATOR. Of course not! Now you must complete these three tasks, and then you'll be ready to save the world. First, to test your strength, you must open the jar of pickles. To test your logic, solve the Rubik's cube, and finally, to test your perseverance, you must punch the teddy bear!

BETH. *(confused)* Ummm..........okay.

*(***BETH** *starts doing her tests like they are the easiest things in the world to do, which they are. While she does this,* **MR. NARRATOR***, well, narrates)*

MR. NARRATOR. While what's-her-face trained vigorously, she learned many things about herself. What her talents really were.

*(***BETH** *finishes her 'tests'.)*

BETH. Umm.....I'm done.

MR. NARRATOR. Babs was now ready to start on her journey.

BETH. *(ticked off because* **MR. NARRATOR** *got her name wrong again)* IT'S BETH! If you want me to do this, you gotta get my name right. Oh, and another thing, I just realized that in the time it took me to do those lame tests of yours and you to narrate, you probably could have gotten over to the *(does air quotes)* "real hero's" house, and already be on your way.

MR. NARRATOR. Nonsense! And besides, don't you want to be a hero?

BETH. Not really, no. I just want to go to sleep.

MR. NARRATOR. Well, you don't have a choice in the matter, now just let me narrate and you just do what I say. *(to audience)* And now folks, our fearless hero was ready to get going. She was so excited to be a hero. She couldn't even think about sleeping at a time like this.

BETH. Actually, I CAN think about–

MR. NARRATOR. *(interrupting)* Even if she did want to go to bed, she wasn't even near a bed.

BETH. *(puzzled)* What are you talking about? My bed is right there! *(points to bed)*

MR. NARRATOR. *(to* **BETH***)* Not for long!

(Lights flash, the **GUYS IN BLACK CLOTHING** *come onstage waving their arms, and take away the set, until it was just* **BETH** *alone onstage.)*

BETH. *(to* **GUYS IN BLACK CLOTHING** *as lights are still flashing)* WOAH! who are you? What are you doing? Hey! That's my bed!

(Fed up, **BETH** *quickly takes her cell phone off of the bed stand that is being carried away.)*

That's it! I'm calling the cops!

(One of the **GUYS IN BLACK CLOTHING** *grabs the phone from* **BETH***'s hand.* **BETH** *is in shock and can't find words.* **GUYS IN BLACK CLOTHING** *go offstage without speaking.)*

Scene 2: IN THE ABYSS

BETH. *(finding her voice, angry)* WHAT THE HELL WAS THAT ALL ABOUT?

MR. NARRATOR. They work for me. Never mind them though. *(to audience)* We find our hero in "The Abyss," where she will learn about her arch foe.

BETH. "The Abyss"? You mean an empty area in space where there is only me and nothing else? I could get used to that! *(yawns)* Perfect for sleeping in. All I need now is a pillow and a blanket.

MR. NARRATOR. Hey! There is no sleeping here. This is where you must learn about your foe, so you can defeat him!

BETH. *(has had enough)* NO! I have had it! I'm leaving! You've had your fun, I'm outta here! *(starts to leave, but then freezes and a look of terror comes on her face)* What's going on? How come I can't move?

MR. NARRATOR. *(disappointed)* Now look what you've made me do, Beulah. Why couldn't you just do as I said? I don't like taking away free will, but I had no other choice.

BETH. *(scared)* You took away my free will? How?

MR. NARRATOR. Yes, I did. I thought I made it clear that I have complete power. Watch this!

(**BETH** *stands straight, dance music starts playing,* **BETH** *then starts doing a dance.*)

BETH. *(still dancing)* Let me go! I'll do as you say! I promise!

MR. NARRATOR. Fine, but next time you pull a stunt like that again, it's adios free will!

(**BETH** *moves her arms and legs to make sure she can control herself.*)

Now, do as I narrate.

BETH. *(scared and uneasy)* Yes, of course.

MR. NARRATOR. *(pleased with this new sense of respect)* Great. Our hero starts reading an ancient text about her arch nemesis–The Evil Carl!

(The generic "Dun Dun Dun" sound effect plays. This happens anytime the words CARL or CARL CAVE are mentioned. At first, **BETH** *will be surprised by it, but by the last 'Dun, Dun, Dun',* **BETH** *will get very annoyed with it. Yes, it is going to get very irritating.)*

BETH. *(laughing, but still a little uneasy)* CARL?! Oh, that's rich! That doesn't sound so evil to me. And where is this "ancient text" I am supposed to be reading.

(A large book slides across stage, and **BETH** *picks it up. It is an encyclopedia.)*

An Encyclopedia? Seriously? Okay, whatever you want, boss man. *(starts reading to self)* Copyright 2005? Yeah, real ancient all right. *(continues reading)*

MR. NARRATOR. *(to audience, while* **BETH** *reads to self)* Betty learned much information about her foe.

BETH. *(frustrated)* MY NAME IS BETH!

MR. NARRATOR. His strengths, his weaknesses and such. Soon she was ready *(quietly, to* **BETH***)* Are you ready?

BETH. *(sarcastically)* Oh sure! I mean according to this description, he has no weaknesses. He's about seven feet tall, strong as an ox, a black belt, and is a super genius. Bring it on! *(rolls eyes)*

MR. NARRATOR. EXCELLENT! Our hero is ready to begin battle with the Evil Carl in the location of his lair, THE CARL CAVE!

BETH. *(bursting into laughter)* THE CARL CAVE?! You're kidding, right? That wasn't in the book! Wow. How imaginative. I just love the alliteration.

MR. NARRATOR. Our hero was at the Carl Cave in a flash!

*(***BETH*** laughs hysterically at the name again.)*

Scene 3: THE CARL CAVE

*(The **GUYS IN BLACK CLOTHING** come on again, as well as flashing lights. They bring a desk, a laptop, a swivel chair, they also scatter a few pizza boxes on the floor and give **BETH** a foam dart gun. Lights come up, and **CARL** is sitting at his desk downstage right, back to **BETH**. laughing maniacally to self while typing on his laptop. The laptop has stickers on it, such as heavy metal bands or super heroes. There is a foam dart gun on desk as well as a small net, a box of **CARL**'s super shake mix and a sweet collection of assorted action figures. A mattress is on the floor upstage center, which acts as **CARL**'s bed.* **NOTE:** *CARL is NOT seven feet tall, not muscular, definitely not a black belt, he is a super genius but lacks common sense.)*

CARL. *(unaware **BETH** is in room, to self)* Soon, I will be ruler of this world! Those unsuspecting people will bow down to worship me! *(**CARL** starts typing quickly on his laptop.)*

MR. NARRATOR. Our hero snuck up behind her foe as quietly as a ninja.

*(**BETH** examines the foam dart gun in her hands, confused, then starts to sneak up on **CARL** like a ninja, but kicks a pizza box by accident and freezes.)*

CARL. *(quickly turns towards **BETH**, surprised)* Who's there?

BETH. Umm…hi. I'm uh, Beth. I'm here to stop your reign of…terror?

CARL. I knew Mr. Narrator would send somebody to try and stop me eventually! By the way, how did you get in here?

BETH. I really don't know. There were flashing lights and then some sketchy looking people in leotards came, and then I guess I just wind up wherever Mr. Narrator says.

CARL. Oh. Well, that makes sense. But what doesn't make sense is why he sent a kid. Isn't it past your bedtime?

BETH. *(shaking her head)* You have no idea. (**BETH** *examines* **CARL**) So, you're Carl?

(**CARL** *nods.*)

You see, I wasn't too sure, because the description I read about you said you were a black belt, muscular, and like seven feet tall, and you're obviously not that, and…*(pauses and smells the air)* Eww! Gross! is that mold I smell?

CARL. Maybe a little. Mother hasn't been down to clean yet. She does it every month. But to confirm your previous statement, yes, I'm Carl. Obviously, the description and information you have on me is false. The government wrote it, and as I'm sure we both know, they never get anything right. I am flattered though, and yes, you are standing in The Carl Cave!

BETH. Hold the phone, your MOTHER? Please tell me that this place *(laughs)* The Carl Cave, is not the basement in your mom's house.

CARL. *(defensive)* Of course not!

CARL'S MOM. *(from offstage)* CARL! Do you want any hot cocoa?

CARL. *(embarrassed, cringing)* NO, MA!

CARL'S MOM. *(offstage)* Are you sure? I can put those tiny marshmallows you like so much in it!

CARL. *(angry)* NO THANKS, MA! LEAVE ME ALONE! *(sheepishly, to* **BETH***)* Okay, so maybe I live in my mother's basement, but she is oblivious to my doings.

BETH. Yeah…okay. Can we just get this over with? *(yawns)* I really need to get to sleep.

(**BETH** *takes aim with her foam dart gun, and* **CARL** *picks up his own foam dart gun, which is on his desk and he aims it towards* **BETH**.)

MR. NARRATOR. Beth took aim with her foam dart gun and Carl did the same with his and they each fired!

(**BETH** *dodges* **CARL**'s *foam dart, but* **CARL** *gets hit with* **BETH**'s *and makes an over dramatic scene.*)

CARL. Ow, that kinda tingled there for a sec, but I am not out for the count!

MR. NARRATOR. Carl had been unfortunate enough to get shot but was not out for the count!

CARL. Let's see how you like this! *(throws a small net onto **BETH** that is on desk)*

BETH. *(sarcastically and monotone)* Oh darn. An easily escapable net. Whatever shall I do? I guess I'll just wait for my demise.

CARL. *(oblivious to sarcasm)* Yes, girl! and now that you're trapped, I might as well tell you my plan!

BETH. Actually, that would be quite nice, since I still have no idea what you were trying to accomplish. I only know that I was supposed to stop you. You see, I didn't have such a great teacher.

MR. NARRATOR. *(upset)* Hey!

BETH. *(to **MR. NARRATOR**)* What? It's true! Now, shut up! I think I kind of need to hear this!

MR. NARRATOR. Brittany listened carefully to Carl's devious plan.

BETH. *(in a fit)* Once again, I tell you, it's BETH!

MR. NARRATOR. *(mocking **BETH**)* Shut up! I think you kind of need to hear this!

CARL. Anyway, my plan is to hypnotize people over the internet and make them buy my new diet shakes.

*(Two **SHOW GIRLS** come onstage, pick up the box from the desk and act like Vanna White wannabees, as if it were some glorious prize, and a game show theme is played. The box is labeled "Carl's Super Awesome Diet Shakes.")*

The diet shakes actually make you five pounds heavier with each glass.

(At this point, another person comes on stage from downstage right who has a shirt that is obviously stuffed to make him look fat. He waddles and then falls over himself and slowly drags himself offstage downstage right, but not before taking a peek in one of the pizza boxes strewn across the floor and then taking it with him.)

CARL. People will be so big and fat, they won't be able to move! I will be the only thin person. I would be able to control everybody, because nobody would be able to stand in my way. Literally! And to make things even sweeter, I am going to overcharge everyone for the shakes, so I'll also be rich!

BETH. *(unenthusiastic)* Is that it? That's what all the fuss is about? I'm not sleeping right now because I need to stop some diet shake scheme?

CARL. *(proud of himself)* Yep. Pretty genius, don't you think?

BETH. More like pretty stupid.

CARL. Shut up! I didn't ask for your opinion

BETH. Actually, you kinda did.

CARL. Well, I don't care! It's a good idea!

*(Pouting, **CARL** turns his back to **BETH**.)*

BETH. *(fake pity)* Well, I'm sure that it's a fantastic idea, and I just don't appreciate it, but I've had just about enough of this crap.

MR. NARRATOR. And with that, Bella ripped through the net with her strength and started hand-to-hand combat with Carl!

*(**BETH** gently takes off net, and instead of hand to hand combat, she grabs and pulls on **CARL**'s ear.)*

MR. NARRATOR. I guess that works too.

CARL. *(**CARL** drops his shake box, in pain.)* OW!!!

BETH. Listen up Carl, you're going to stop this so called 'evil' plot of yours. You may be a super genius, but you're also an idiot!

CARL. NEVER!

*(**BETH** pulls on **CARL**'s ear harder.)*

AHH!!! Okay, okay! you win! I'll stop!

BETH. Promise?

CARL. *(sobbing)* Yes, I promise!

BETH. Good. But just to make sure....

(**BETH** *knocks laptop to floor, and it breaks.* **BETH** *lets go of* **CARL**'s *ear, who rushes over to laptop and starts to cry.*)

CARL. *(on his knees holding his broken laptop, mourning as if he had just lost his best friend)* LAPPY!!! NO!!!

BETH. *(pitiful)* That's just pathetic.

MR. NARRATOR. The world is safe once more, thanks to the abilities of Bree!

BETH. *(irritated)* FOR THE LAST TIME, MY NAME IS BETH, YOU MORON! B-E-T-H, BETH!

MR. NARRATOR. *(uptight)* That's what I said.

BETH. Whatever, can you just take me home now? *(yawning)* I need to go to sleep.

MR. NARRATOR. Of course young hero, you deserve it!

BETH. *(relieved)* Great.

MR. NARRATOR. Our hero was bushed from spending all night fighting evil, and now she was ready for her journey home.

(*Lights flash,* **GUYS IN BLACK CLOTHING** *come on for the last time. They move the Carl Cave set offstage, and one of them takes* **CARL**, *and he cries on their shoulder and gets consoled and they bring back the set for* **BETH**'s *room. The clock now reads 3:45 am.*)

Scene 4: BACK IN BETH'S ROOM

BETH. Well that was certainly...fun? Well, goodbye Narrator man, wherever you are. I hope we never cross paths again.

MR. NARRATOR. Goodbye to you too. Get some rest young hero, you're going to need it.

BETH. *(climbs into bed, turns off lights)* Whatever! Go away! GOODNIGHT!

(Three seconds of silence in the dark.)

MR. NARRATOR. We find our hero resting peacefully yet again, unaware that she had to save the world one more time that night!

BETH. *(quickly, turns on light and gets out of bed)* Oh, no, no, no! I don't think so bud! I am done! *(to audience)* I guess there is only one solution to get my way. *(in the same annoucer-esque voice as Mr. Narrator)* Our hero was seriously pissed off and was going to teach Mr. Narrator a lesson! *(storms offstage)*

MR. NARRATOR. Hey, what are you doing, where did you go? Oh hey, buddy! How did you get up here? Hey, don't look at me like that! Ow, that hurts! Stop that! That doesn't bend like that!

(The sound of masking tape and then some muffled shouting, then nothing. **BETH** *comes back onstage, brushing her hands off, a smile on her face.)*

BETH. *(exhausted)* Screw the world, I'm going to sleep. *(Gets into bed, turns off light and closes eyes.)*

End of Play

PRODUCTION NOTES

CASTING: The role of Beth doesn't necessarily have to be played by a chick. Beth's name. can easily be changed to the name Ben if the role is given to a dude. Some of Mr. Narrator's lines would obviously have to be changed if this happens, including, but not limited to all the mistakes of the name he makes as well as changing the words from feminine to masculine. Screwed up names Mr. Narrator uses are just any name close to the name of the character that is short and starts with a 'B', such as Butch, Bob, Bill, Brad, and Bo. The Guys in Black Clothing can also be cast as The Gals in Black Clothing as needed. They can also be double cast at the Show Girls and the Fat Guy.

OTHER NOTES: Remember, as mentioned in the script, ANYTIME the words 'Carl' or 'The Carl Cave' are mentioned, the stereotypical evil bad guy 'Dun Dun Dun' sound needs to be played. This includes ridiculous moments when it wouldn't make any sense for it to be played like when Carl's mother calls his name. The sound should be played at that point too. If the sound effect is not available, use voices from backstage.

As far as profanity goes, it may not be suitable for some audiences, and the language may be edited out and changed as necessary.

www.ingramcontent.com/pod-product-compliance
Lightning Source LLC
Chambersburg PA
CBHW052029290426
44112CB00014B/2439